Sunshine and Dewdrops

Dr. Aftab Ahmed

ISBN

Hardcase 979-8-89415-281-3
Paperback 979-8-89363-358-0

For my children,
Shiara, Yaseen and Farhan

Life will throw you many challenges, be the best you can be.

CONTENTS

ACKNOWLEDGMENT AND GRATITUDE

I begin with my gratitude to almighty Allah for bestowing his blessings, guidance and wisdom upon me. I would also like to express my heartfelt gratitude to my dear family and friends. Your unwavering support, love, and encouragement have been my pillars of strength throughout my journey.

To My Parents: Thank you for your sacrifices, wisdom, and unconditional love. You've shaped me into the person I am today, and I am forever grateful.

To My Wife, Reshma: Your patience, understanding, and companionship have made every moment worthwhile. Thank you for being my partner in this beautiful adventure called life.

To My Children Shiara, Yaseen and Farhan: You are my joy, my pride, and my greatest achievement. Your laughter and innocence light up my world. Thank you for being my little stars.

To My Friends: Your camaraderie, laughter, and shared memories have enriched my life beyond measure.

From the bottom of my heart, thank you all for being a part of my journey.

FOREWORD

Sunshine and Dewdrops: A Journey through Photo verses and Quotes

"Sunshine and Dewdrops" is not just a book; it's a visual and poetic journey that invites readers to find solace in the beauty of the world around them. Each photo image is a window into a moment of time and feelings, while the accompanying verses and quotes distill the essence of the image into words that resonate with the soul.

The book is a celebration of the simple yet profound moments that life offers. It reminds us that hope can be found in the smallest of things—from the delicate dew clinging to a blade of grass to the warm rays of the sun breaking through a cloudy sky. These are the instances that refresh our spirit and offer a sense of renewal.

In essence, this book is a collection of reminders that no matter what challenges we face, there is always a glimmer of hope waiting to be discovered, and a fresh start just around the corner.

May this book of photo verses and quotes bring a ray of sunshine and a touch of dew to your day, filling it with hope and the freshness of new beginnings.

1 CARPE DIEM

Down and lost, I slept through my anguish,
And then, I saw the dewdrops glistening in the morning sun.
I asked, "Hey dewdrop, isn't your life evanescent, yet you see seem so happy?"
She smiled unto me, and said,
"My dear, I live in the moment. Seize the moment, nothing else matters!"

2 THE FLIGHT

If you set your mind free from the prison of your thoughts,
And believe in your heart, no flight is impossible.

3 HOPE

When you embrace pain, and choose hope every time,
You stand apart and glow like sunshine.

4 CHALLENGE

I burst the bubble of mundane life,
I began to rise again,
And challenged myself to an unknown height,
I embraced the story of my life,
And so, I began to rise again,
This time determined not to give up without a fight.

5 PERSEVERANCE

If Moon can move the oceans from a distance,
Who can stop you from moving the earth with your persistence?

6 ADAMANTINE

Keep the soft heart pristine; don't let the travails of life harden you,
Keep the spirit to fight for right; don't let the gloss of wrong dishearten you,
Keep the light within to shine, don't let the dark nights eclipse you,
Fall my dear, but rise and shine again!

7 WILDFLOWER

It is easy to bloom with beautiful people around you,
Your mettle is when you blossom like a wild flower in unusual places.

8 INDOMITABLE

Your courage and perseverance will define,
Your journey to transform, sparkle and shine!

9 BORN TO FLY

There is no height you cannot scale in the sky,
If you firmly believe that you are born to fly.

10 BELIEVE

Don't wait for a falling star to brighten your dark night,
You are the star, believe in your light!

11 I AM RIGHT HERE

I wish you scale dizzying heights, but if you cannot,
Like a harness to control your fall,
My dear, I am right here.

12 TRANSFORMATION

A Butterfly is beautiful, but not before the caterpillar breaks through its cocoon, Transformations are painful, yet they shape you into something magnificent.

13 ENOUGH

In this overwhelming infinite cosmos,
If you believe in yourself, YOU are enough!

14 PHASES

A full moon is beautiful, but not before it goes through its phases,
It doesn't matter if life breaks you; it also shapes you in stages.

15 LIMITLESS

Sky is not your limit,
Your limit is defined by your heart, mind and soul,
And each one is different.

16 RISE

Rise, my dear!
The rose in you is stronger than the thorns that break you.

17 STARDUST

You don't need light in the darkness,
My dear, you carry the stardust of the cosmos,
Wherever you go, you will sparkle!

18 BROKEN BUT BEAUTIFUL

I see the dark clouds in the sky,
As they thunder, and pour raindrops weeping,
I realize how delicate they are to embrace,
Broken, yet not losing their grace.
Broken doesn't mean it is the end,
We are still left with the many pieces,
Though broken, much more beautiful.

19 HEALING TOUCH

A tryst with nature changes everything,
When you see the majestic beauty of Sunset,
When you feel the stoic music of cool breeze,
When you hear a soothing melody of silence,
You can sense the rhythmic dance of your joyful heart,
And you know that nature has come alive and will heal any broken soul.

20 NOT WITHOUT A FIGHT

Even in the abyss of despair,
Promise yourself, not to give up without a fight,
Is it not in the darkest of nights, the stars shine brightest?

DARK BETWEEN THE STARS

Life wouldn't be meaningful if we don't embrace its *beauty along with the scars,*
Just as the night sky wouldn't be charming if not for the *dark between the stars.*

22 SHINE

And one day, I decided I would stand up to Sun,
And declare, "I too am going to rise and Shine."

23 MERAKI

When you create something, put your heart and soul into it,
When you are gone, a part of you will always remain in your work,
The only things that stay forever are those forged by love and passion.

24 SCARS ARE BEAUTIFUL

I am beautiful because of my scars,
They are my strength,
A proof of my defining struggles,
My will to survive anything,
A reward that stayed with me when most left.

25 PHOENIX

I don't fear fire; I rose from the ashes,
I chose to create, nurture and forgive,
I can give light to brighten the darkness,
But be warned, if needed, I can burn everything to oblivion!

26 NOT DONE YET!

I may fall, fail and break on my way to top,
But will also recoup, rise and not stop,
I am not done yet!

27 DEWDROPS

Dewdrops falling on me,
I no longer felt alone,
I broke the shackles free,
Touched the peak and claimed the crown.

28 YOUNIVERSE

Only when you seek and leave your *Youniverse*,
You can truly see and embrace the beauty and magic of this universe.

29 STUBBORN HEART

Everything you love,
Everything you dream,
Everything you seek,
Will find its way to you,
Just believe, persist and pursue my dear,
The universe will bow and bless a sincere heart.

30

CHILD OF COSMOS

Live as if you are a child of the Cosmos,
Believe everything is destined for you, every star shines for you.

31 LIGHTHOUSE

In the most inclement of weathers,
I wish you stand bravely like a light house,
Battling the tempest with resilience,
And guiding the lost with your indomitable spirit.

32 LIFELINE

If I pass through a struggle, you are my strength,
If I doubt myself, I see your faith,
If I see my success, I feel your pride,
And if I live a dream, you are my lifeline!
I wish I can be to my son, what you are to me as my father.

33 LOVE WILL FIND YOU

She asked, "Where will I find love?"
She heard back, " You don't find love my dear, love will find you, and you will know it at the right moment."

34 MANGATA

Just like the beautiful mangata of moon,
Love in its true essence will always mirror love.

35 LOVE

A heart full of love is like a garden with flowers,
You share it and it blossoms forever.

36 RAINBOW OF LOVE

If life is a tapestry of eclectic colors layered with joy and sorrow,

Its love that makes it complete with its beautiful rainbow.

37 POWER OF LOVE

Sometimes love is the only thing left to hold on,

And yet, love is enough!

38 LIGHT IN HEART

Let your heart awaken to its light,
And bring sunshine even in the darkest of the night.

39 LOOK INSIDE

Sometimes what you seek outside is always within you,
Open the window to your heart,
The light you see there is brighter than the sunshine.

40 GRATITUDE

To someone who lives under the cold snow, the morning gleam of sunlight is a marvel,
To someone who lives in the harsh desert, the overhanging clouds are magical,
Life is beautiful when we cherish what we have than live in anticipation of what it can be.

41 DECLUTTER

If you have to rediscover yourself, you have to let go,
Only when you declutter, you redefine yourself and grow.

42 LET GO

I see the shed autumn leaves dancing away, and waving goodbye,
Then I see the beautiful spring come to life with new leaves blooming,
It's a perfect balance between letting in, and letting go.

43 INNER CHILD

Don't let your mature philosophy of life overshadow your child like curiosity and wonder.

44 THE SECRET

The mundane is in believing what you see,
The magic is when you start seeing what you believe,
If you believe in good, you will see good happen,
The secret of this magic is not around you, it's in *you*!

45 EMBRACE LIFE

I stood in the garden of happiness, hoping to forget my sorrows,
I realized that it takes rain and sunshine to blossom the flowers,
When I embraced my sorrows wholeheartedly,
I found that happiness had never left me.

46 SOUL FOOD

I asked her, "What makes you happy?" She replied smiling,
"Sunrise that quells the night of its darkness,
Dewdrops that brings a wave of freshness,
Zephyr that soothes my tense skin,
Woods that rejuvenates my tired mind,
Stars that shimmer and light up the night sky,
Moon that steals the night with its celestial beauty,
And people who are magical with their words and deeds. They are my soul food."

47 SPIRAL OF LIFE

Life is a spiral of good and bad, joy and sorrow,
It doesn't change; we get better dealing with it each tomorrow.

48 THE TRIALS

Just as moon goes through its phases to become complete and beautiful,
Life tests us with different challenges to makes us resilient and indomitable.

49 FAITH

I asked, "I am alone, am I enough?"
I heard back, "My dear, what if Sun felt alone, and stopped shining?"

50 HOME

I went around the world in wanderlust,
Only to return, and find my heart at home.

51 ROOTS

Isn't it beautiful to grow, branch and blossom,
Yet remain grounded to your roots?
The wings can take you anywhere,
But heart will bring you back home.

52 SEEDS OF LOVE

In this ephemeral life, the only thing eternal is love,
Plant love and see how it blossoms and beautifies this world.

53 EARTH-HEART

If the word EARTH could be rearranged into a most beautiful word, it would be HEART, Listen to the voice of Earth, she needs people with loving heart !

54 PANACEA

Happiness is infectious, but spread it freely,
A happy heart is a panacea for any malady.

55 GIVE YOUR LIGHT

The Moon shines beautifully with Sun's reflected light,
Yet, Sun never feels jealous of Moon's glory,
When you love someone, you give all your light and let them shine.

56 FORGIVE

Verily, is it not a beautiful heart which loves and forgives easily?
For its ability to love is beautified even more by its capacity to forgive.

57 EXPRESS LOVE

She said, "I don't like your long poetry. Express your love in one verse."
I smiled and replied, "You are my entire universe!"

58 MON AMOUR

In my life, like memorable moments,
In my sleep, like beautiful dreams,
In my death, like a comforting end,
You shall remain in me and with me forever,
It's a promise, we shall keep together!

59 LOSS

Love and loss are the fabric of life,
If you love, you will also lose,
If you don't, then you are lost,
So live, love and loose,
For the joy of love has power to heal the grief of loss.

60 FRIEND

Ever felt sad, lost and alone? And in your solitude looked up at the dark sky?
Did you not find a perfect partner there?
The beautiful Moon, looking back at you intently?
Not asking you any questions, not imploring you for any answers,
Not judging you in anyway,
Just listening to you quietly, and shining,
For sometimes, what you need is not someone who talks brilliantly, but a friend who listens to your heart silently.

61 AGE WITH GRACE

Age is not a curse but a gentle embrace,
A journey of wisdom laced with serene grace.

62 TRUE BEAUTY

In the dance of time, as moments unfurl,
With passing age, beauty does twirl,
True beauty resides within the heart,
With a light that shines, never to depart.

63 TAPESTRY OF LIFE

Life is a tapestry of different colors,
It's beautiful because nothing lasts forever!

64 HAPPINESS KNOCKS THE DOOR

Happiness comes knocking your door when you keep,
A blissful heart that sees good in everything,
A serene mind not perturbed by adversity,
And a bunch of cheerful good friends.

65 A PERFECT BALANCE

When your mind is at peace, and heart at ease,
Your life will be in perfect balance.

www.ingramcontent.com/pod-product-compliance
Lightning Source LLC
LaVergne TN
LVHW071148160826
845679LV00003B/595

* 9 7 9 8 8 9 3 6 3 3 5 8 0 *